Collins

INTERNATIONAL PRIMARY ENGLISH

AS A SECOND LANGUAGE

Student's Book 4

Contents

About this book

This magazine-style Student's Book provides a wide variety of resources for classroom use and general enjoyment which act as the main stimulus (or "input") for the *Collins Cambridge Primary English as a Second Language* course. The modern presentation has been carefully designed to get the learners interested and involved in the learning process and to provide stimuli for discussion. The main aim is to make language learning both engaging and enjoyable, and to get learners thinking about themselves and the exciting world they live in.

You will find stories, short articles, poems, picture-dictionary pages, puzzles, maps, simple graphs and photographs linked to the topics for the year. The rich and varied visual resources provide interest and encourage oral communication and deeper thought about the topics.

Learners are guided through the material by clear, simple instructions which tell them what to read and give prompts for what to else to do.

You will notice that there are coloured bubbles with small symbols on many of the pages.

This tells you that there is something to **talk** about.

This tells you that there is something to **think** about.

There are many opportunities for learners to talk about the materials. Talking should be encouraged, and learners should not be afraid to talk about what they can see and what they have read. Talking about their ideas allows them to use the language they are learning and improves their confidence and fluency. Sometimes they will need to use their mother tongue when sharing their ideas, experiences and deeper thoughts. This is a natural part of fluency development and should not be received negatively. Allow learners to express themselves fluently and confidently in the mother tongue, and then support them with the vocabulary they need to say it in English too!

Above all, learners should be enjoying their learning as this develops a positive and inquisitive approach to the world around them and their place within it.

The authors

Time to relax

**We asked some children what they do in their free time.
Read what they said.**

Naeem's report

Free time is fun time. It is not time to do homework or chores. I like to be active in my free time. I play tennis and I go swimming. Sometimes I go for a hike with my dad. He is very fit and he makes me walk very fast. Sometimes I am lazy and I spend my free time watching TV. I love watching shows about nature and science.

Nina's report

Free time is quiet time for me to relax. I like to spend my free time on my own. I sit at my desk and play computer games. Sometimes I play against my friend, Desi, but other times I play on my own. I also like to read and draw. If it is cold and rainy I jump into bed and read books or magazines.

How do you like to spend your free time? Do you prefer to be alone or spend time with others?

Interesting hobbies

Read about two interesting hobbies.

A hobby is something that you enjoy doing in your free time. Some people bake, some people paint and some people build models as their hobby. What do you do?

ToyVoyagers – travelling toys

A ToyVoyager is a toy that you send on a journey around the world without you. To do this as a hobby, you choose a toy and register it on the ToyVoyager website. Each toy is given a special travel tag and an identity number. Once you are registered, you give the toy to someone who is going on a journey. They take photos of your toy in the places they visit and send the photographs and some information to the ToyVoyager site. They later give the toy to someone else to take on a different journey. The toys travel all over the world in this way. You can share your toy's adventures by checking the ToyVoyager website. There are more than 3,000 toys taking part and some have been travelling for many years.

Geocaching (say "jee-oh-cah-shing")

Geocaching involves hunting for hidden containers, called geocaches. The containers are hidden in interesting places in the environment. People who take part are given GPS information which they use to find geocaches hidden in different places. When you find one you open the container and take the small treasure found there. You leave a new treasure for the next person and write your name and other details in the log book. Then you put the geocache back so other people can find it. Geocaching takes place all over the world. This hobby is a fun way for families to get into the outdoors and learn more about places around them.

Where would you hide a geocache in your area? Why do you think that is a good place?

A Hike in the Park

Listen and follow.
Then read the poem again on your own.

What things can you see when you go on a hike?

Last week I went for a hike in Forest Park.
I packed a torch in case it got dark.
I packed my sweater and my lunch,
In case I needed something to munch.

But as I walked, I heard a strange sound –
A shuffle, a scuffle, but when I turned round
There was absolutely nothing there
Just bright green grass and clear fresh air.

I walked on and up. I jumped over rivers.
I kicked down a rock – it gave me the shivers.
For what if the rock knocked somebody flat?
I really, truly wouldn't want that!

Still, every so often, I heard a strange sound –
A shuffle, a scuffle, but when I turned round
There was absolutely nothing there
Just bright green grass and clear fresh air.

I walked behind a small waterfall.
And luckily for me, I'm not very tall.
So I kept myself safe and stayed almost dry
I'm glad the waterfall wasn't that high.

Still, every so often, I heard a strange sound –
A shuffle, a scuffle, but when I turned round
There was absolutely nothing there
Just bright green grass and clear fresh air.

I emptied my bag of paper and peels
And all the remains of all of my meals.
I put all my rubbish into the bin
And closed the lid. It made quite a din.

Then as I walked off, I heard a strange sound –
A shuffle, a scuffle, but when I turned round
This time it seemed there was something there!
I'm quite sure I spotted a massive brown bear!

By Jennifer Martin

Games around the world

Read about how to play different games from around the world.

People all over the world play different games. Have you ever heard of 'Gonggi nori' or 'Keeper of the Fire'?

Gonggi nori

Gonggi nori is a game from Korea played with five small stones (or metal pieces, in a cross shape, called jacks).

To play, you throw these onto the ground and then you pick one up and toss it into the air.

You have to quickly pick up another stone from the ground, and catch the one you tossed into the air *before* it lands.

If you manage it, you move straight onto the next round … you pick up *two* stones, toss them into the air and try to pick up another two and catch the two in the air, before they land. You carry on like this, tossing up and grabbing three stones, then four.

In the final round you toss *all five* stones into the air and try to catch them *on the back of your hand*. The number you manage to catch is your final score. If you don't manage to grab and catch the correct number of stones each round, the next player gets a turn to try.

This game is played in many different countries around the world.

Keeper of the Fire

This is a traditional Native American game where children try to remove sticks from the 'fire keeper' without getting caught. One person is chosen to be the fire keeper. The fire keeper sits in the middle of a circle with a pile of sticks next to them. They must wear a blindfold and keep their hands in their lap. They are not allowed to move their hands until they hear a raider taking sticks. The other players quietly sneak up to the fire keeper and try to remove one stick from the pile. If the fire keeper hears the raider, they can move their hands. If they touch the raider, the raider becomes the fire keeper.

Do you play any games that are similar to these?

Word games

What word games do you know?
Here's one you can play at school or at home.
Read the rules. Play the game with your group.

The same-letter word game

1. One person starts. He or she says a word or a person's name.

2. The next player has to find words to describe the word or name that is given. These words must begin with the same letter as the word or name.

3. Players get one point for every correct word they give.

4. If a player cannot think of a word, the next player in the group gets a turn.

5. The first player to get ten points is the winner.

Why do games need rules? What happens when someone doesn't follow the rules?

Ball.

Bouncing blue ball.

Carol.

Clever, caring Carol.

In the rainforest

Read this brochure to learn more about rainforests.

Rainforests are found near the equator in Africa, Asia, Australia and Central and South America. The largest rainforest in the world is the Amazon rainforest. Rainforests are damp and humid places.

Join us on one of our spectacular rainforest tours!

My name is Carlos. I'm the guide for the night walking tours. If you want to go on an adventure of a lifetime, the rainforest is for you!

- *You will learn about nature.*
- *You will get up close to plants and animals.*
- *You will make new friends and you will be left with wonderful memories!*

What is the rainforest like?

Rainforests have four levels. Our tours take you through the understory layer. You will look up to the canopy and also examine the forest floor as you walk through the understory layer.

The tall canopy is like a roof of branches and leaves very high above the forest floor.

The floor is dark and damp because very little sunlight reaches it. Most of the floor is covered with rotting leaves and other decaying vegetation.

What animals live there?

Each level of the rainforest is home to different kinds of animals.

Monkeys, frogs, lizards, birds, snakes and sloths are found in the canopy and emergent layer.

Bigger animals such as forest elephants, tapirs, jaguars and leopards live in the understory layer.

Lots of insects live on the floor. This is also home to giant anteaters.

What happens after dark?

At night the rainforest really comes alive.

All the bats wake up. They like to fly in the dark. They hunt moths and insects. A hungry bat will eat hundreds of insects in a night.

Would you like to take a walk through a rainforest at night? Why? / Why not?

Lightning bugs wink and shine like little lights. A lightning bug will flash its light on and off to say it is looking for a mate.

Snakes slide and sneak up on their food. Lots of snakes come out at night. Some hunt on the ground. Some slither up trees. Some snakes eat tree frogs. They can see in the dark. If they see a frog, they sneak up and grab the frogs in their mouths.

This is a tree frog. It has sticky fingers to help it climb trees and it can see in the dark too. It looks for moths, grasshoppers and small insects to eat.

Grasshoppers climb in the trees at night. They feed on plants. They have long feelers to help feel their way in the dark. Frogs, bats and tarantulas eat grasshoppers.

Bugs Are Helpful

Read the poem to learn how bugs can be helpful.

Bugs!
We're everywhere.
We're in the water,
We're in the air.
Indoors, outdoors, underground,
Wherever you look that's where we're found.
We're on your hands and in your hair,
We're with you in the clothes you wear.
Bugs!
We can make your tummy funny,
Or a thousand noses runny.
Got a cut? Get a plaster.
Keep us out and you'll heal much faster.
We're the ones who make you ill,
Because of us you take that pill.
We're the ones who make you mad,
By turning good food into bad.
Bugs!
I agree, we don't sound good.
We cause more trouble than we should.
But … let me tell you this about us,
People on Earth can't do without us.
In fact, you owe us such a lot!
If we weren't here to make things rot …
… the piles of stuff you throw away
Would just get bigger every day.

What good things do bugs do? What bad things do they do?

Yes! We make things rot!
We make them smell!
Apple cores, potato skins,
All the scraps in all your bins –
We get to work and cause decay.
In time we rot it all away.
Rubbish mountains there would be,
If you didn't have my friends and me.
You need plants, and plants can't grow
Unless we're in the soil below.
We go to work on last year's leaves
Making food for next year's trees.
We get to work and cause decay,
In time we rot old leaves away.
Leaf mountains there would be,
If you didn't have my friends and me.
Bugs!
You can't see us,
But how you need us!
Because of all the work we do,
We make life possible for YOU.

By Sam McBratney

Animals from another time

Read about some of the strange animals that lived on Earth a very long time ago.

The Argentine bird or *Argentavis* (say: "ar-jen-tay-vi")

The remains of this huge bird were found in Argentina, in South America. It lived there until about five million years ago.

The Argentine bird was the largest ever flying bird. It was 1.5 metres high. Its wings measured 7.5 metres across. Each wing feather could be as long as 1.5 metres.

This bird ate animals such as lizards, mice and rabbits. It also ate fish.

The Indrik Beast or *Indricotherium* (say: "in-drik-oh-theer-ee-um")

This animal lived in Asia about 30 million years ago. It was the largest ever mammal to walk on land.

The very biggest of these creatures grew to about 4.5 metres high. It had a long neck that made it even taller, so that it could reach leaves high up in the trees.

It was also a very heavy animal. A really big one weighed 15,000 kilograms – that's much heavier than the largest rhino!

The mammoth (say: "mam-oth")

The mammoth was a type of large elephant.

The bones of mammoths have been found in many different places. Those that lived in cold countries had long fur to keep them warm.

Mammoths grew up to three metres high and ate mostly grass and bushes. They had two long tusks which they used to protect themselves from attackers.

These animals are all extinct. What other extinct animals do you know about?

The Terror bird or *Titanis* (say: "tee-tarn-is")

This giant bird lived about two million years ago in North America. It couldn't fly because it didn't have wings, but it did have arms covered in feathers.

This bird stood nearly three metres high and could run very fast. It was a meat eater and hunted small animals, using sharp claws and a very large beak to grip and kill them.

The giant short-faced kangaroo or *Procoptodon* (say: "proh-kop-toe-don")

This animal lived in Australia. It weighed up to 200 kilograms – that's more than twice as heavy as today's biggest kangaroo.

Each of the creature's hind feet had one single large claw, like a hoof. Its long arms could stretch up over its head and its long, grabbing 'fingers' could reach leaves high up on trees. It was able to chew really tough leaves with its strong jaw.

The Great Fire of London

Look at the infographic about the Great Fire of London. Look at the pictures and graphs and read the information to find out about this historic event.

Fire can be very destructive, especially in crowded cities. One of the most famous fires of all time happened more than 350 years ago in the city of London.

FACTS and FIGURES

The fire began in a bakery on Pudding Lane just after midnight on Sunday 2nd September, 1666. It burned for nearly four days.

87 out of **109** places of worship burned down.

80%

4/5 of the city was destroyed

+/- 500,000 people lived in London in 1666

The city was very dirty and dry.

Many people were sick as a result of the plague.

There was not enough piped water.

People had to use buckets to try and put out the fire.

THE BUILDINGS

The houses were made out of wood and straw.

They were built close together.

The streets were very narrow and crowded.

Some houses were four storeys high.

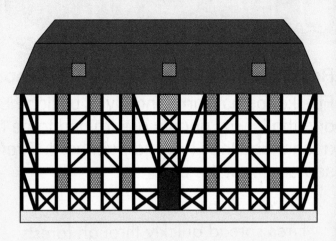

THE RESULT

+/- 100,000 people lost their homes

6 people died

It took nearly 50 years to rebuild the city.

1666   1706

The new buildings were made of brick and stone.

Besides people and animals, what three things would you save first if there was a fire? Why?

Firefighters

Read about firefighters and the important work they do.

Fire keeps us warm and gives us light. But fire can be dangerous …
and that's why people are trained to be firefighters. Firefighters work as
a team and they have to train hard. Firefighters put out fires on land, at
sea and from the air.

Forest fires

Fires spread quickly through forests.
Helicopters water-bomb forest fires.
Fortunately, the forests will grow again.

Will forests always grow again?

Blowout!

An oil well fire can burn like a huge, flaming torch. This is called a blowout.

Would you like to be a firefighter? Why? / Why not?

Fire at sea

Firefighters use jet skis to put out fires on small boats. Jet skis work in shallow water. Big oil tanker fires need fire boats with powerful hoses.

Chemical fires

Firefighters use foam to fight chemical fires. The foam stops smoke from spreading.

Fire safety!

1. Don't play with matches and lighters. If you see matches or a lighter lying around, tell an adult.

2. If there's a fire in your house, GO OUTSIDE! Although fires are scary, NEVER hide in cupboards or under beds when there is a fire.

WAY OUT

3. If there's a fire, FALL and CRAWL. It is easier to breathe in a fire by staying low.

4. If your clothes are on fire, STOP, DROP and ROLL on the ground until the fire is out. Shout for help, but do not run. Running makes the flames burn faster.

5. Always have an escape route and practise using it. Check to see that doors and windows can open easily in case there is an emergency.

6. Choose a meeting place outside. NEVER go back into a burning building. If someone is missing, tell the firefighters. They have the right clothing and equipment to rescue people.

Fire Safety Rules

7. Know your emergency number.

What to do if there is a fire drill

- When you hear the alarm, stay calm and listen to instructions.
- Stop what you are doing and leave everything on your desk.
- Line up quickly. Don't run and don't push.
- Follow your teacher outside to the meeting point.
- Stay with your class at all times.
- When your teacher tells you it is safe, go back to class in an orderly fashion.

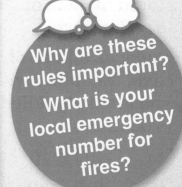

Why are these rules important?

What is your local emergency number for fires?

Puff, the Dragonsaurus

Dragons are known as brave creatures who breathe out fire. But they weren't always like that. Read this story to find out how they learned to do this.

Once upon a time, long, long ago, before the Moon was the Moon and the Sun was the Sun, a family of dragonsauruses (dragons for short) lived in a cave. The dragons were rather shy and they were scared of many things. They hid away from mice. They ran away from butterflies. They trembled when they heard the wind blow. In fact, most days they didn't leave their cave.

One cold, gloomy autumn day, the family of dragonsauruses woke up to the sound of an enormous crash. Worriedly, they peeped out of their cave. And what an incredible sight met their eyes – there, outside their cave, stood a terrible beast. It stared at them and shouted loudly, "Hey! You! Get lost. This is going to be my cave!"

Quick as a flash of lightning, the dragons fled to the back of their cave, trembling with fear. "Oh what are we to do?" cried Mother. The family huddled in the back of the cave, trying to work out what to do next.

"Er… Can I help?" asked Puff, a young dragon in the family.

"Hush, Puff," replied his father, "only grown-ups can solve this problem. You do want us to be safe, don't you? Just sit quietly. Go and read a book."

But Puff decided he was not going to read a book while his family was in danger! He turned around and crept out of the cave. Luckily, the beast was tired after all the shouting and was sleeping soundly. Puff crept carefully past it and ran as fast as the wind down the hill.

When Puff stopped to catch his breath, he looked up and saw an old tree.

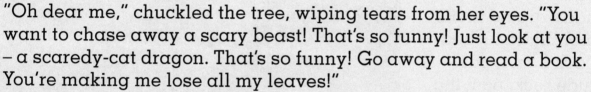

"Excuse me," said Puff, "but do you know how to chase away scary beasts?" That made the tree laugh so much that many of her leaves fell off her branches.

"Oh dear me," chuckled the tree, wiping tears from her eyes. "You want to chase away a scary beast! That's so funny! Just look at you – a scaredy-cat dragon. That's so funny! Go away and read a book. You're making me lose all my leaves!"

And so Puff continued his journey sadly. He was feeling tired and thirsty by now, so he stopped next to a river and sat on a rock. "Oi!" growled the rock crossly. "Get off me!" Puff got such a fright he leaped into the air and nearly landed in the river!

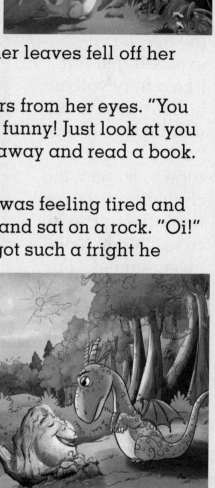

"What are you doing here?" demanded the rock, rudely. "Dragons never leave their cave."

Puff told the rock all about the scary beast and the unhelpful tree. "And you think you can help chase the beast away?" laughed the rock, loudly. "Dear, dear me! That's so funny! Go away. You're making me laugh so much that I'm starting to crack! The tree was right – go and read a book."

Poor Puff sighed deeply. Would he ever be able to help his family? Would he ever be able to come up with a plan to chase away the monster? He decided to walk just a little further along the path before turning back to go home. A shiny berry on a bush caught his eye. It was red and sparkled like a ruby. Puff had never seen such a berry before (which was not surprising considering that he'd always stayed close to the cave). Curiously he picked it. Carefully he licked it. It didn't have a taste. Then he smelled it. It didn't have a scent. "Is it safe to eat?" he wondered. Puff was so hungry he decided he'd take a bite. After all, what harm could one teeny tiny bite do?

Well, it did a lot! Puff thought his tongue was exploding. It felt like a fiery volcano had erupted in his mouth! He rushed back home, past the rude rock, past the chuckling tree, up the hill, back to his cave. "Mom! Mom!"

he screamed. "I'm ..." Puff stopped. To his complete amazement, fire was coming out of his mouth. He turned in shock and looked at the beast which by now was wide awake.

The beast's eyes grew wide with fear when it saw the flames coming from Puff's mouth. "Help!" it screamed as it ran away. "I'm being attacked by a fire-spitting dragon!"

And that's how Puff saved his family. It's also how dragons learned to breathe fire and become brave enough to leave their caves.

By Jennifer Martin

What type of story is this? How do you know it is not true?

Peter and the Wolf

Look at the pictures. What do you think happens in the story of Peter and the Wolf? Listen to this play script of the story, and follow along.

Peter and the Wolf is a traditional story about how a boy and his friends managed to outsmart a wolf that wanted to eat them.

NARRATOR: Peter lived with his grandfather in a small cottage near a forest. In front of the cottage lay a big, green meadow. Peter ran into the meadow and met his friend, Bird.

BIRD: Tweet! Hello, Peter. Have you come to play with me?

PETER: (bravely) No. I'm going into the forest to catch the big, bad wolf.

(A duck comes waddling into the meadow.)

DUCK: Quack! Quack! Don't go into the forest, Peter. Come and have a swim with me.

BIRD: TWEET! What kind of bird are you if you can't fly?

DUCK: Quack! Quack! What kind of bird are you if you can't swim?

BIRD: TWEET! TWEET!

DUCK: QUACK! QUACK!

PETER: Don't be silly. Duck's in the middle of the pond and you can't swim.

NARRATOR: Bird and Duck were arguing so much, they didn't see Cat come creeping up. Cat pounced at Bird …

CAT:	Grrr! MIAOW!
NARRATOR:	... but Bird flew up into the branches of a tall tree.
BIRD:	Nah, nah, nah-nah, nah! You can't catch me.
CAT:	Miaow! Well, I'll climb the tree and get Bird. (Cat stares at Bird at the top of the tree.)
NARRATOR:	Suddenly, Grandfather ran into the meadow, waving his arms. He looked very cross.
GRANDFATHER:	(angrily) Peter! I told you not to play in the meadow. It's a dangerous place! Go back home and stay there!
NARRATOR:	As soon as Peter and Grandfather had gone, a big, grey wolf came creeping out of the forest.
WOLF:	Ha ha ha! Peter's gone. Now I can catch my dinner! (The wolf creeps up on Cat.)
NARRATOR:	When Cat saw the wolf she jumped up into the tree.
CAT:	MIAOW! MIAOOOOW!
NARRATOR:	The wolf ran over to the pond. Duck saw the wolf, so she waddled out of the pond and tried to run away through the forest.
DUCK:	QUACK! QUACK!
WOLF:	Yummy! Duck dinner for me!
NARRATOR:	The wicked wolf snapped hold of Duck's tail ... and with one big gulp, he swallowed her up.
WOLF:	GULP! Slurp! Slobber!
NARRATOR:	High up in the tree, Cat and Bird looked down at the wolf. The wolf looked up at them.
WOLF:	(licking his lips) Yoo-hoo! I'm coming to get you too.

NARRATOR: But Peter had seen everything. He climbed out of his bedroom window and ran into the forest, carrying a strong rope.

PETER: (whispering to himself) I'm going to teach that wicked wolf a lesson.

(Peter scrambles up the tree where Bird and Cat are sitting.)

PETER: (in a low voice) Bird, go and fly around the wolf's head until he's sick and dizzy. And keep him near the bottom of the tree!

(Bird flies round and round the wolf's head.)

BIRD: WHEEEEEEE!

WOLF: Oi! Silly Bird. Go away. You're making me dizzy.

(Peter makes a lasso out of the rope, and dangles it down until it slips over the wolf's tail.)

NARRATOR: The wolf didn't see Peter … but he felt the lasso when it was pulled tight round his tail.

WOLF: OWW! What's that! Get off my tail!

(Peter ties the end of the rope round the thick branch he and Cat are sitting on – still high in the tree.)

PETER: Ha ha! I've got you, you big, bad wolf.

NARRATOR: Just as Peter had tied up the wolf, a hunter came out of the forest and pointed his gun at Bird up in the tree.

PETER: Don't shoot! Bird and I have caught the big, bad wolf.

HUNTER: Amazing! Let's take him to the zoo.

The Pied Piper of Hamelin

Look at the pictures. What do you think happens in the story? Then listen to the story. Did you predict what happens correctly?

The Pied Piper of Hamelin is a traditional story with a lesson. The story teaches that it is important to keep your promises.

Help! The Sky Is Falling

Do you know the story of *Chicken Licken*? Read the poem with a partner. Take turns to read.

Chicken Licken was out one day,
Minding his business, I must say,
When a little acorn fell on his head
Chicken Licken thought he was soon to be dead!

"The sky is falling – the end is near,
I must tell the queen – that is clear.
I must tell the queen, and the king too,
For they'll know exactly what to do."

So off he hurried and soon met a friend
He told Henny Penny that the world would soon end.
"Cluck cluck, Oh no – that cannot be,"
Said Henny Penny seriously.

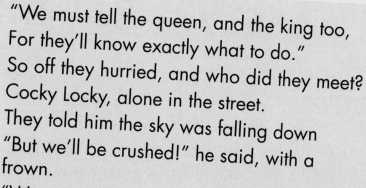

"We must tell the queen, and the king too,
For they'll know exactly what to do."
So off they hurried, and who did they meet?
Cocky Locky, alone in the street.
They told him the sky was falling down
"But we'll be crushed!" he said, with a frown.

"We must tell the queen, and the king too,
For they'll know exactly what to do."
Foxy Loxy then walked by.
They told him about the falling sky.
"That's just awful. It's not OK,
Follow me – I know the way."
They followed him high, they followed him low.
He seemed to know which way to go.
Round the corner, then back again,
And straight into the fox's den!

The Foxy family rubbed their tums
They picked their teeth and licked their gums
And that was what happened to that silly bunch
They believed Chicky's story and ended up as lunch.

What do think the lesson is in this story? Why?

Interesting facts about Earth

You probably already know a bit about the Earth. Read this information to learn more about the continents.

Did you know that …

continents are huge pieces of land. There are seven continents today, but long ago they were all joined together. Scientists believe that the continents used to be one large piece of land about 250 million years ago. Scientists call this large continent Pangaea. They believe that Pangaea very slowly broke into pieces to form different continents. The continents slowly drifted apart from each other to where they are today.

Did you know that…

the continents are still moving? Believe it or not, North America and Europe are drifting apart by four centimetres per year. Scientists believe that 50 million years from now, North and South America will have moved apart.

Did you know that…

there are five oceans in the world? The Pacific is the largest ocean. It is bigger than the Atlantic, the Indian, the Southern and the Arctic Oceans put together! The Pacific covers over one-third of the Earth's surface.

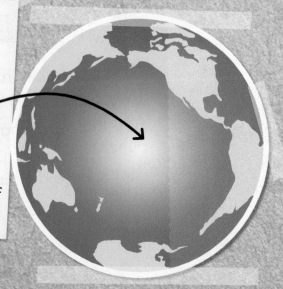

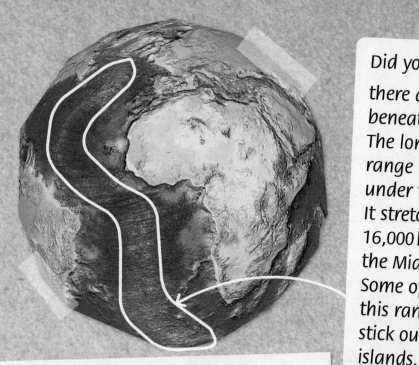

Did you know that …

there are mountains beneath the oceans? The longest mountain range in the world lies under the Atlantic Ocean. It stretches for almost 16,000 km and is called the Mid-Atlantic Ridge. Some of the mountains in this range are so tall they stick out of the water as islands.

Did you know that …

besides a valley in Antarctica, the Atacama desert is the driest place on Earth? It is so dry that in some parts of the desert it has not rained for hundreds of years. Can you imagine living in a place where it doesn't rain at all?

Did you know that …

the Amazon rainforest in South America is the biggest tropical rainforest in the world? The Amazon River flows through the rainforest. The river is the second longest in the world at 6,516 kilometres – only the Nile River is longer. More than 30 million plant and animal species live in rainforests.

Which mountains do you know about? Which is the highest mountain peak in the world? If you don't know, how could you find out?

From stones to skyscrapers – wonders of our world

Which are the most famous structures in the world?

Read the information to learn more about some of the most famous and most visited structures in the world today.

Pyramids are massive ancient stone structures found in different parts of the world. The best known pyramids are the Great Pyramid at Giza in Egypt and the massive stepped pyramid in the Mayan ruins of Chichen Itza in Mexico. No one knows for sure how pyramids were built with basic equipment thousands of years ago, as the stones used to build them are so big that engineers would struggle to move them today with modern equipment.

Petra is a famous city carved out of a stone cliff in Jordan. It is also called the Rose City because the sandstone it is carved from has a pink colour. Petra was the capital of the Nabataean empire of King Aretas IV who ruled from 9 BCE to 40 CE. The people of that time used technology wisely, and built huge tunnels and water chambers. They also built a theatre for 4,000 people!

The Colosseum in Rome is the largest stone amphitheatre ever built. It was originally built to celebrate the glory of the Roman Empire. Nearly every modern sports stadium is based on the Colosseum's original design with its stepped seating and many numbered exits. Many cruel fights and games took place in the arena, watched by over 55,000 spectators.

The Great Wall of China is the largest monument ever to have been built by human hands. It is not actually one wall, though. It is a series of walls joined by forts and other structures that was built and added to over a 2,000 year period. The wall is over 20,000 km long, and it is said that it can be seen from space (although astronauts on the International Space Station have said they could not see it). The Great Wall was originally built as a military barrier to protect China from invaders.

Machu Picchu is known as the city in the clouds. It was built in the 15th century, on the high slopes of the Andes Mountains in Peru. Historians believe that this massive city was built by the Inca Indians and later abandoned because of an outbreak of smallpox. The ruins were rediscovered in 1911, and today thousands of people climb the more than 3,000 steps to visit this amazing place.

The Taj Mahal at Agra in India is a more modern monument. This huge tomb is a famous example of Islamic art and architecture. It was designed in 1632 to honour the memory of the emperor's late wife. The tomb is built from white marble and surrounded by beautiful walled gardens and water features. More than three million people visit it every year.

In 2017, the Burj Khalifa in Dubai in the United Arab Emirates is the tallest structure in the world. The Burj, which was opened in 2010 is 829.8 m tall and 160 storeys high. It is surrounded by high buildings but it towers over them. Levels 125 and 148 are observation decks and visitors are whisked upward in glass elevators in just a few seconds to get amazing views of the surrounding area.

If you could choose three of these places to visit, which would you choose? Why?

Amazing places

People have built many wonderful things, but there are also many amazing natural places on Earth. Read about some of the natural places Li and her family have visited.

Amazing places we've been to

Last year we went diving in the Komodo National Park in Indonesia. We also saw huge Komodo dragon lizards! I was surprised that they were so big!

This is the underground river at Palawan in the Philippines. The river flows through a huge cave. We went into the cave on a boat and learned about the cave and the animals in the national park.

Table Mountain is in South Africa. When the wind blows in a certain direction, the clouds cover the top of the mountain just like a table cloth! More than 1,430 different plants can be seen at this site. We went to the top of the mountain in a cable car that turns around as it goes up.

Can you imagine cruising on a boat down the Amazon River! We did this for three days in a houseboat. The Amazon River flows through the largest rainforest in the world, and carries more water than the ten largest rivers in the world combined. That's a lot of water!

Ha Long Bay is in Vietnam. It is a huge bay. More than 1,900 small islands are found in the bay. Some of the islands are hollow caves. Many fishermen live in floating villages among the islands. Some of the islands are so big that they have their own lakes!

The Iguassu Falls are made up of 275 separate waterfalls. The falls are 2,700 m wide. Part of the Iguassu Falls are in Brazil, and the rest is in Argentina. We saw some amazing birds and a rainbow.

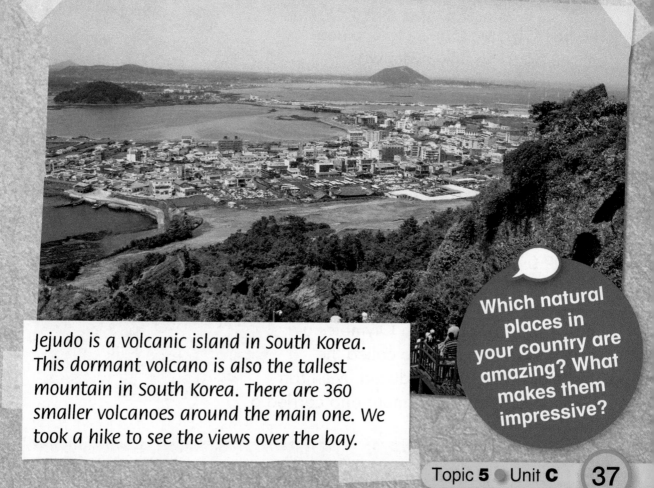

Jejudo is a volcanic island in South Korea. This dormant volcano is also the tallest mountain in South Korea. There are 360 smaller volcanoes around the main one. We took a hike to see the views over the bay.

Which natural places in your country are amazing? What makes them impressive?

The Olympics in ancient times

What do you know about the history of the Olympic Games? Read the information below to find out more.

http://www.historyofolympics.com

The first ever Olympic Games took place in 776 BCE – more than 3,000 years ago! The ancient Olympic Games were very different to the modern ones we have today. The Olympic Games get their name from the ancient site of Olympia where the first games were held. Olympia was an important meeting place for the Greeks. The ruins of ancient buildings can still be seen at the site today.

One day! One race!

The first Olympic Games took place on one day. The only event was a short running race from one end of the stadium to the other. The track was rough and wide and 20 people could run at the same time. Only men who spoke Greek were allowed to take part in the games.

Over the years, other events were added, and the games took place over four days. The events included wrestling, boxing, javelin and discus as well as horse and chariot races. At the 65th Olympics a really tough running race called the hoplitodromos was introduced. Men ran this race in full sets of armour and carried a heavy shield.

There was only one winner in each event, and there were no gold, silver and bronze medals like we have today. The winner was given a wreath made of olive leaves as a prize and a statue was built in his honour.

Winners became very famous. One of the most famous Olympians was Leonidas of Rhodes. He won all three of the running races at four games in a row. He became a hero of all the Greeks.

The first woman to win an event was Kyniska of Sparta who won the chariot racing event. However, she didn't actually take part in the Games! The rules said that the winner was the owner of the horse, not the rider.

The Olympics became very important in ancient Greece. At that time, Greece was divided into city-states, and they were often at war with each other. But the Olympics were so important that the city-states stopped all their battles and held a special truce for a full month before the Games started so athletes could train in peace. The Olympic Games were held regularly at Olympia until they were banned by a Roman emperor in 393 CE.

Why do you think the Roman emperor banned the Olympic Games? Are the Olympic Games popular in your country? Why? / Why not?

From ancient to modern

Read the information below to learn more about the modern Olympic Games.

Baron Pierre de Coubertin was a Frenchman who thought it would be good to restart the Olympic Games. The first modern Olympics were held in Athens, Greece, in 1896 and they now take place every four years in different host countries. Athletes from all over the world take part in the modern Olympic Games. Their achievements are watched by millions of people both at the events and on TV. Women competed in the Olympic Games for the first time in 1900.

The Olympic flag has five intersecting rings. Each ring is a different colour: red, black, green, blue and yellow. The rings represent the Americas, Australia, Africa, Asia, and Europe and how they come together in the Olympic Games.

The Olympic torch is a symbol of the ancient Greek Olympic Games. The flame is lit in Greece a few weeks before the Games and it travels around the world to the host city. It usually is carried by runners, but in 2000, the torch travelled underwater for the first time when a diver took it past the Great Barrier Reef in Australia.

Originally, the Olympics were only held in the summer. The first Winter Olympics were held in 1924, in Chamonix, France. In the Summer Games, athletes compete in around 30 different sports: on the track, on the road, on grass, in the water, on the water, in the open air and indoors. The running sprints are very popular. The Winter Games consist of seven sports that take place on snow and ice, both indoors and outdoors.

To be selected for the Olympic Games is the dream of most athletes. They spend hours training and make many sacrifices to achieve their goals. The athletes that qualify for the Games are among the best in the world, and even if they do not win a medal, they are called Olympians.

Athletes who take part in the Olympic Games have to agree to be tested to make sure they have not used any banned medicines that might give them an advantage. These tests are called doping tests and they are carried out before and during the Games. For individual sports, such as athletics, tests are performed on all the athletes who are placed in the top five in any event. Two random athletes in each event are also tested.

Why are doping tests important?

Going for gold!

Read about the first gymnast who got a perfect score in an Olympic event.

Nadia Comaneci

Nadia Elena Comaneci is a famous gymnast from Romania. She was good at gymnastics from a very young age, and she started training for the Olympics when she was just six. Even though she was so young, she was expected to train for four hours a day, six days a week. Can you imagine spending 24 hours a week doing intensive training?

In 1976, at the age of 14, Nadia Comaneci stunned the world at the Montreal Olympic Games. Her performance was so good that she received seven perfect 10 scores, and won three gold medals. Nadia became the first gymnast ever to score a perfect 10 in an Olympic gymnastics event. But the scoreboard couldn't show 10. It could only show up to 9.9, so they showed her score as 1.0, not 10.0!

When she participated in her second games in 1980, Nadia won another two gold and two silver medals.

After a long and successful gymnastics career, Nadia Comaneci retired from the sport of gymnastics in 1984. She now lives in the USA with her family.

What were you doing when you were six years old? What do you think Nadia's childhood was like?

Read about the incredible swimmer, Michael Phelps, who is the most successful Olympian of all time.

Michael Phelps was only 15 years old when he participated in his first Olympic Games in Sydney, Australia, in 2000. He still had braces on his bottom teeth, and remembers that he didn't take the Games seriously enough. But that didn't stop him from starting a brilliant swimming career! He finished fifth in the 200 m butterfly, but for him that wasn't enough. He wanted to be the best in the world.

"There are reasons why I swam every holiday, every Christmas, every birthday. I was trying to be as prepared as I could, and I tried to see what I could really do and what my potential was. I just really did kind of whatever it took. I dreamed of doing something that no one had ever done before."

Michael Phelps has competed in three Olympic Games. He has a total of 22 Olympic medals and is the most successful Olympian of all time!

Phelps decided to retire after the Games in Rio de Janeiro in 2016. Now, he is helping his coach, Bob Bowman, to train younger swimming stars. He is not sure what else he will do in the future. With his drive and commitment, he's sure to be successful, isn't he?

How do you think it feels to win an Olympic medal?

Seeing and listening

Read about the senses we use every day to make sense of our world.

Our senses are in action from the day we're born, and we use our senses to explore and learn about the world around us. We have five sense organs – eyes, ears, skin, nose and tongue. Sense organs are connected to the nervous system.

Everybody has the same five senses, but some people's senses are better than others. For example, some people can see really well, and others can hear very soft sounds.

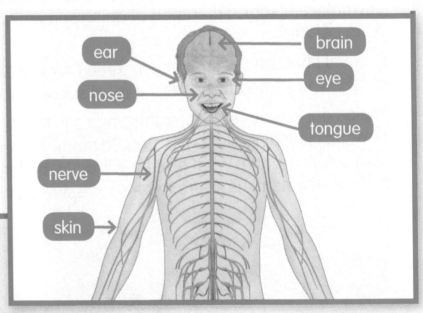

- ear
- nose
- nerve
- skin
- brain
- eye
- tongue

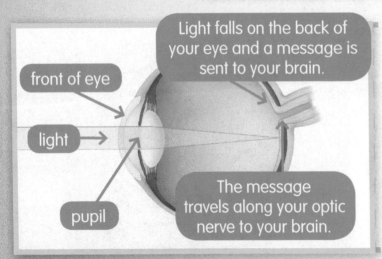

- front of eye
- light
- pupil

Light falls on the back of your eye and a message is sent to your brain.

The message travels along your optic nerve to your brain.

Humans can see in colour. Many animals see only in shades of black and white.

But, humans can only see colour when there's lots of light. If we go outside at night, we can only see in black and white.

Sounds are made when something vibrates (moves). For example, a guitar makes a sound when you pluck the strings.

Your ears hear the sounds and send them into a tube called an ear canal. They reach your eardrum and make it vibrate. The vibrations pass to your cochlea (say: "kok-lee-uh"). This is a tube that looks like a snail's shell. Inside your cochlea, liquid moves tiny hairs that send messages along nerves to your brain.

Your ears help you to balance. When you move your head, liquid inside the semicircular canals moves too. At the same time, your eyes are sending information to your brain. Your brain uses all this information to move your arms and legs and stop you falling over.

When you spin around, lots of messages from your eyes and ears are sent to your brain. Your brain gets confused and you feel dizzy.

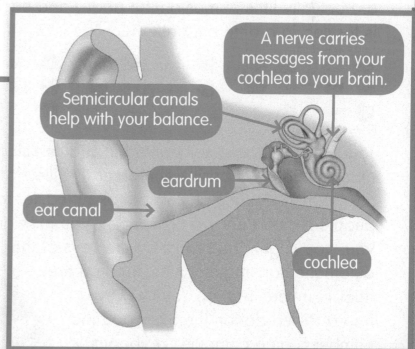

A nerve carries messages from your cochlea to your brain.

Semicircular canals help with your balance.

eardrum

ear canal

cochlea

Which sense do you think is the most important? Why?

Braille – reading by feeling

Robert loves reading. However, Robert is blind, so he reads a special alphabet called braille with his fingertips. Read what he says about reading in braille.

You read braille with your fingertips. The letters are actually little bumps on the page, and each letter is formed in a different pattern.

Today, many books are printed in braille using a special machine called a braille embosser. Braille signs are also found in public places to make it easier for blind people to find their way around. If you look around you, you might find braille on the keys of the automatic banking machines and on the floor numbers in a lift. You may even find a raised dot on the J key and the number 5 on a computer keyboard.

I read my school books in braille, but I also listen to audiobooks, and my mom often reads aloud to me. I really enjoy that.

At my school we use special computer programs to help us. The keyboard has braille letters and the programme speaks the words on the screen. So, if I type in an email, the computer reads it out as I type so that I can check my work. When I go to a website, the computer reads out the text on the screen.

Some people are legally blind. This means they are not completely blind but they can see very little. They sometimes read special books with very large print. Electronic readers also help them as they can make the print as big as they need it.

Think about what it is like to be blind or to have low vision. How do blind people do everyday things?

Helen Keller

Read about Helen Keller and her achievements.

1880

1880 Helen is born in Alabama in the USA. She starts talking at the age of six months.

1882 Helen gets a fever and becomes blind and deaf.

1885 Her parents do research to try and help their daughter.

1887 Anne Sullivan, a teacher, comes to live with the family to teach Helen to communicate with others.

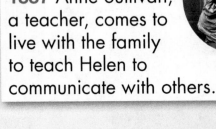

1890 Helen goes to speech classes at a school for deaf children.

1902 Helen writes her first book, *The Story of My Life.*

1904 Helen is the first deaf and blind person to graduate with distinction from college.

1920 Helen works hard to tell other people about deafness and blindness, and to help others. She travels and writes more books and is awarded several degrees.

1920

Helen Keller was born on June 27th, 1880, in Tuscumbia, Alabama. She grew up on her family's large farm which was called Ivy Green.

She was not born blind and deaf; at nineteen months old she became very sick and lost her hearing and her sight. For a child this was very frustrating, and Helen became very angry when she could not communicate with her family. She kicked and screamed. But Helen did not give up. She communicated with her family in her own way using signs. When she wanted to say that she was cold, she would shiver.

"The best and most beautiful things in the world cannot be seen nor even touched, but just felt in the heart."   *Helen Keller, 1891*

When Helen was six years old, Anne Sullivan came to stay with Helen's family as her teacher. Anne wanted to teach Helen to communicate but it was not easy to do. One day, Anne let water run over Helen's hand. Then she traced w-a-t-e-r on Helen's hand. Helen understood – the letters spelled 'water'. Helen learned many other words that day!

Helen learned to read books in braille. She also learned to write and speak. She used a special typewriter to write her first book.

Helen wanted to go to college. She attended Radcliffe College (Harvard University), and Anne Sullivan went with her to help her to do well at the college.

Helen Keller lived to be 88 years old and she spent her life helping people to understand about deafness and blindness. She also helped many other deaf and blind people learn to communicate.

How do you think Helen Keller felt as she was growing up?

Blackbeard the pirate

In the past, many sailors became pirates in the hope of becoming rich. Blackbeard is one of the most famous pirates of all time. Read Blackbeard's life story.

Blackbeard the pirate was born in England around 1678. His real name was Edward Teach, but he was called 'Blackbeard' because he always grew a long beard. He used to tie ribbons on the ends of his beard! Although everyone was very scared of him, Blackbeard never killed anyone.

Before he went into battle to loot a ship, Blackbeard would dress smartly in black clothes. He would fasten some guns to his chest and wear a large, black captain's hat. Then he would put slow-burning fuses in his beard and hair. The fuses gave off smoke, which covered Blackbeard in a thin blanket of fog. This made him look so scary that many captains gave up their ships without a fight!

Blackbeard and his men sold the goods they stole. People didn't report him to the authorities because the stolen goods were cheap and they bought them even though they knew this was against the law.

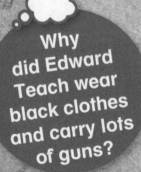

Why did Edward Teach wear black clothes and carry lots of guns?

Some facts about pirates

- 💀 Pirates believed that piercing their ears would improve their eyesight.

- 💀 Pirates believed that whistling on a ship would turn the weather stormy.

- 💀 The pirate flag is called the Jolly Roger.

- 💀 Pirates sometimes hid their treasure so no one could find it. Blackbeard's treasure was so well hidden that, even after he died, no one ever found it. Divers have found his ship, and have brought up many items such as cannons, other weapons and tools, but no treasure! They didn't even find a treasure map, so Blackbeard's treasure is still hidden somewhere!

The Map

the ship

the river

the cave

the Pirates

the hill

the trees

the beach

Can you see where the treasure is buried on this island?

Treasure Island

Treasure Island tells the story of Jim Hawkins, a young boy who goes on an adventure to find buried treasure. Look at this book review for *Treasure Island*.

BOOK REVIEW
Treasure Island

Author: Robert Louis Stevenson

Length: 232 pages

Publisher: (Various); first published in 1883

Genre: Fiction

Language: English

Rating: ★★★★★ 5/5 Stars

Treasure Island is an exciting, classic adventure story, which I couldn't put down! I heartily recommend everyone should read it, regardless of their age!

Do you like adventure stories? In *Treasure Island*, why did Jim want to get away from the sailors on the beach?

Here is part of the story. Read it with a partner.

Treasure Island looked scary. There were a lot of trees and rocky mountain peaks. Even though it was a sunny day, I did not feel happy.

Our ship was anchored in a small bay. The air was still and heavy and the men were cross and restless.

Captain Smollett told the men that they could go ashore which made them much happier! They were excited to go and look for buried treasure. Long John Silver, the ship's cook, was put in charge of the men. I had nothing else to do, so I decided to go with them.

When we got ashore, I went on my own. I ran up the beach to the trees. It felt good to be on my own for a while. I sat quietly, hidden by the bushes. But then I heard voices. I quietly moved closer to hear the words more clearly. I saw Long John Silver bullying one of the sailors. He wanted the sailor to join him and the other sailors and go against Captain Smollett! Long John Silver was double-crossing the captain!

I knew I was in great danger. I ran away from the scene as fast as I could. I didn't care where I went as long as it was as far away from Long John Silver and the other sailors as possible!

I stopped to rest at the foot of a rocky hill. But then I saw a movement out of the corner of my eye. What was it? Was it a man? Was it an animal? I felt very scared, so I changed direction and headed for the beach. The creature was faster than me, and darted from tree to tree. It came closer and closer. Then I saw what it was - it was a man, a wild man! When he got near to me, he fell to the ground and held up his hands as if he was begging for mercy. He was dressed in rags, and his skin was tanned dark by the sun.

Buried treasures

One of the most famous tombs ever discovered belonged to a young pharaoh called Tutankhamun. Read about some of the treasures found in his tomb.

Do you remember reading about the pyramids in Egypt? These were special chambers to bury Egyptian pharaohs. But not all pharaohs were buried in pyramids: most of them were buried in hidden chambers cut into the rocks at a place we now call the Valley of the Kings. This was to keep the burial places secret so no one tried to steal the valuable treasures buried with the pharaohs.

Today, the tombs in the Valley of the Kings have been dug out and there are clear paths and entrances for tourists. In the early 1900s, this area was rocky and sandy and almost all of the tombs were buried under layers of rock and sand. Some were underneath old houses and other buildings.

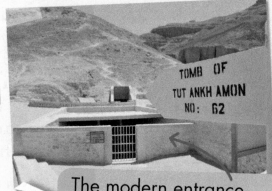

The modern entrance to Tutankhamun's tomb in the Valley of the Kings.

A small tomb with a massive treasure!

In 1922 an archaeologist called Howard Carter made an amazing discovery in the Valley of the Kings. After searching for six years, he found a stone step under the remains of old huts. He dug further in the sand and then he found some stairs. At the bottom of the stairs he found a door which turned out to be the entrance to Tutankhamun's burial chamber.

Inside the tomb, Carter found the undisturbed burial chamber with Tutankhamun's mummified body and rooms filled with treasure.

Tutankhamun is known as the 'boy pharaoh'. He was only nineteen when he died. He was buried in one of the smallest tombs in the Valley of the Kings.

The ancient Egyptians believed that their kings needed to be buried with their belongings. Tutankhamun was buried with bottles of oil, perfumes, statues and gold jewellery. There were also chariots, chairs, model boats and paintings! It took Carter and his team 10 years to make a list of all the things in the tomb.

The most expensive coffin in the world?

King Tutankhamun's mummy was found inside a set of three special coffins. The two outside ones were made of wood covered with thin gold foil. The inside coffin was made out of solid gold. It weighs 110.4 kilograms and would cost millions of dollars to make today.

Today, you can visit the burial chambers in the Valley of the Kings, but the treasures have been removed. You can see these at the Egyptian Museum in Cairo, where all of the treasures from Tutankhamun's tomb are displayed in a special exhibition room.

Models of everything in the Tutankhamun exhibition travel around the world for special shows. Why do you think they don't use the originals?

Anjali's diary

Read Anjali's diary about her holiday.

Anjali and her family went on a safari in Africa. It was the first time that they had seen animals in the wild and they enjoyed their holiday in the game reserve.

Look at the zebra patterns carefully. What differences can you find?

Home	Insert	Design

B *I* <u>U</u> abc X₂ X² A A A ≡ ≡ ≡ ≡

Monday

Today we met our tour guide, Jabu. He knows a lot about animals. He took us on a game drive to a water hole. We had to sit very quietly in the Land Rover so that we did not scare the animals away.

Jabu told us that every zebra has its own striped pattern and that they sleep standing up. Now I understand why zebra crossings in towns and cities have their name!

Tuesday

Today was very cloudy and windy, so I took a blanket with me in the van. We left for our game drive very early this morning. Everyone was yawning and sleepy, but not for long! Jabu took us deep into the bush and we were lucky enough to see a lot of animals. Jabu stopped the Land Rover and told us to keep very still. He stared at a tree. I thought he was being silly, but when I looked carefully, I saw a beautiful leopard lying fast asleep on a branch. Not many people get to see a leopard in the wild!

Wednesday

We spent most of the day at the campsite because it was too hot to go out on a drive. Jack and I made friends with some of the other children. We had lots of fun swimming in the pool. One of the little girls was being very naughty and kept on splashing us! There were lots of monkeys in the trees. Some of them had babies. I liked watching them.

Thursday

Jabu took us out for a hike today. We saw many different plants and trees. We also saw a bright green snake! We had to drink lots of water and wear hats and sunblock.

Friday

Today was our last day. I was feeling sad because I had not yet seen a lion. It was my dream to see the king of the wild. We went for our last drive, and there, on the side of the road, we saw a lioness and her cubs. They were so sweet! I took a lot of photos!

Which wild animals would you most like to see? Where could you see them in the wild?

Island fun

Adverts try to convince you to buy something by making it sound attractive. Read this advertisement for a summer holiday.

Call us today on 123-234-5678 or visit our website
www.islandhoppers.sun
Special offers for early bookings. Don't wait. Don't leave it too late!

Sun, Sand and Sea – it doesn't get better than this!

Relax in the sun.
Dig in the sand.
Play in the clear blue sea and swim
with dolphins.

Leave the shopping centres behind.
Make new friends. Learn to surf. Catch fish.
Collect shells.
Have the best time ever!

Island Hoppers can make this happen.

How does this advert try to make the holiday sound good?

A day on an island

Look at the children having fun on the island. Read what the children are saying.

Where would you go?

Read the text messages these children sent their friends. Can you work out which country each person is visiting?

I'm sending you this message from the very top of the Eiffel Tower. It is amazing up here and you can see the whole city. We're going to the Louvre Museum tomorrow.

It is really amazing here. The sun shines for about 22 hours every day. It hardly gets dark at all. There are reindeer here and we went on a boat on a fjord yesterday.

I'm near the top of the boot-shaped country. We went to visit the Leaning Tower of Pisa, it really does lean over. I took a photo that looks like I am holding it up.

If you could go anywhere in Europe, where would you go? Why?

You'll never believe where I've just been. It is the largest stone amphitheatre ever built and modern stadiums are still built in this style. Can you guess?

Read these two poems about different cities in Europe.

Paris

Glittering, Busy

Rushing, Twinkling, Driving

Taking photos of the Eiffel Tower

Posing, laughing, clicking

Walking, shopping, waiting

Beautiful, fashionable

City

Look at the poems again. What is the structure of the poems?

Barcelona

Bright, Exciting

Walking, staring, smiling

Admiring amazing buildings

Feeling lost quite often,

Directions, maps

Home

An imprint of HarperCollinsPublishers
The News Building
1 London Bridge Street
London SE1 9GF

HarperCollins Publishers
1st Floor
Watermarque Building
Ringsend Road
Dublin 4
Ireland

browse the complete Collins catalogue at
www.collins.co.uk

© HarperCollinsPublishers Limited 2017

10 9 8 7 6 5 4 3

ISBN 978-0-00-821367-1

British Library Cataloguing in Publication Data
A catalogue record for this publication is available from the British Library.

Author Jennifer Martin
Publisher Celia Wigley
Commissioning editor Karen Jamieson
Series editor Karen Morrison
Editor Alexander Rutherford
Project managed by Tara Alner
Edited by Tracy Thomas and Cassandra Fox
Proofread by Zoe Smith
Cover design by ink-tank and associates
Cover artwork by Jane Ray
Internal design by Ken Vail Graphic Design
Typesetting by Ken Vail Graphic Design
Illustrations by QBS
Production by Katharine Willard
Printed and Bound in the UK using 100% Renewable Electricity at CPI Group (UK) Ltd

Acknowledgements
The publishers gratefully acknowledge the permissions granted to reproduce copyright material in the book. Every effort has been made to contact the holders of copyright material, but if any have been inadvertently overlooked, the Publisher will be pleased to make the necessary arrangements at the first opportunity.

HarperCollins*Publishers* Limited for extracts and artwork from:

Bugs! by Sam McBratney, illustrated by Eric Smith, text © 2010 Sam McBratney. *Animal Ancestors* by Jon Hughes, text © 2006 Jon Hughes. *Peter and the Wolf* by Diane Redmond, illustrated by John Bendall-Brunello, text © 2007 Diane Redmond. *The Pied Piper of Hamelin* by Jane Ray, illustrated by Jane Ray, text © 2011 Jane Ray. *Chicken Licken* by Jeremy Strong, illustrated by Tony Blundell, text © 2007 Jeremy Strong. *The Ultimate World Quiz* by Claire Llewellyn , text © 2008 Claire Llewellyn. *The Olympic Games* by John Foster, text © 2009 John Foster. *Your Senses* by Sally Morgan, illustrated by Maurizio De Angelis, text © 2012 Sally Morgan.

Photo acknowledgements
The publishers wish to thank the following for permission to reproduce photographs. Every effort has been made to trace copyright holders and to obtain their permission for the use of copyright materials. The publishers will gladly receive any information enabling them to rectify any error or omission at the first opportunity.

(t = top, c = centre, b = bottom, r = right, l = left)

p4t bikeriderlondon/Shutterstock, p4b photobyphotoboy/Shutterstock, p5t varuna/Shutterstock, p5b Tyler Olson/Shutterstock, p9 (background t) Lereen/Shutterstock, p9 (background b) atsiana Selivanava/Shutterstock, p9 (letter tiles) Pinone Pantone/Shutterstock, p11b Jim Cumming/Shutterstock, p16 (pie chart) Tikhonov/Shutterstock, p16-17 (background) Marcin Wos/Shutterstock, p18tr Tom Reichner/Shutterstock, p18tl urraheeshutter/Shutterstock, p18br curraheeshutter/Shutterstock, p18bl Lumppini/Shutterstock, p19 lenabsl/Shutterstock, p19br VOLYK IEVGENII/Shutterstock, p30t Niki Whitehorn, p30b Niki Whitehorn/, p31t NGDC, p31c John Warburton-Lee/Alamy, p31b Jon Arnold Images Ltd/Alamy, p32t Mohamed Hakem/Shutterstock, p32b Maciek A/Shutterstock, p33t Lestertair/Shutterstock, p33c SF photo/Shutterstock, p33b SL-Photography/Shutterstock, p34t Fancy Friday/Shutterstock, p34c Alexandra Lande/Shutterstock, p34b Thasneem/Shutterstock, p35t Ethan Daniels/Shutterstock, p35c Nico Wijaya/Shutterstock, p35c (boat) Edmund Lowe Photography/Shutterstock, p35c (diver) SARAWUT KUNDEJ/Shutterstock, p35b Crystal Egan/Shutterstock, p36t Daleen Loest/Shutterstock, p36c lessandro Zappalorto/Shutterstock, p36b PhotoRoman/Shutterstock, p37t Junior Braz/Shutterstock, p37b Narumon Srisirisavad/Shutterstock, p40-41 (background) Petr Toman/Shutterstock, p40t Shahjehan/Shutterstock, p40c Shahjehan/Shutterstock, p40b Ruslans Golenkovs/Shutterstock, p41t Iurii Osadchi/Shutterstock, p41c Leonard Zhukovsky/Shutterstock, p42t Central Press/Stringer/Getty, p42c Bettmann/Getty, p42b AFP/Getty, p43t Leonard Zhukovsky/Shutterstock, p43b Leonard Zhukovsky/Shutterstock, p46-47 (background) Coprid/Shutterstock, p46-47 wavebreakmedia/Corbis Historical/Shutterstock, p48tr Historical/Hulton Archive/Getty, p48br Hulton Deutsch/Archive Photos/Getty, p48bl Topical Press Agency/Stringer/Getty, p49 Fred Stein Archive/Contributor/Getty, p50-51 (background) Andrey_Kuzmin/Shutterstock, p50 North Wind Picture Archives/Alamy, p51 (crossbones) Panda Vector/Corbis Historical/Shutterstock, p53 (background) Valentin Agapov/Archive Photos/Ss/Shutterstock, p54 marco_tb/Shutterstock, p55tr GraphicaArtis/Corbis Historical/Getty, p55tl ALESSANDRO VANNINI/Getty, p55tc ALESSANDRO VANNINI/Corbis Historical/Getty, p55c Orhan Cam/Shutterstock, p55bc ALESSANDRO VANNINI/Contributor/Getty, p55br Hannes Magerstaedt/Stringer/Getty, p56-57, 58 (background) tratong/Shutterstock, p56 GTS Productions/Shutterstock, p57t BlueOrange Studio/Shutterstock, p57b Marci Paravia/Shutterstock, p58tl Doctoresa/Shutterstock, p58tc iSiripong/Shutterstock, p58tr rtmiles/Shutterstock, p58b Rene Blanc/Shutterstock, p59l Brian A. Witkin/Shutterstock, p59c Tory Kallman/Shutterstock, p59r NadyaEugene/Shutterstock, p59 (background) BlueOrange Studio/Shutterstock, p60-61 siraluck/Shutterstock, p62t Thanapong Suthin/Shutterstock, p62ct Svetography/Shutterstock, p62cb Mike Mareen/Shutterstock, p62b Farbregas Hareluya /Shutterstock, p63t Ivan Mateev/Shutterstock, p63tc Sergey Kelin/Shutterstock, p63c auro Rodrigues/Shutterstock, p63bl spatuletail/Shutterstock, p63br s74/Shutterstock